Ghost
of
Revivals Past

Ghost of Revivals Past

Kenneth G Morris

Empowered Publications Inc.
Leroy, Alabama
www.empoweredpublicationsinc.com

On the cover: 1. Evan Roberts 2. D. L. Moody 3. Jack Coe 4. T. DeWitt Talmage 5. Bud Robinson 6. William J. Seymour 7. John G. Lake 8. John Alexander Dowie 9. Smith Wigglesworth

© 1996 Kenneth G. Morris
All Rights Reserved
Scripture Quotations are taken from the Kings James Version

Published by Empowered Publications Inc.
26812 Highway 43
Leroy, Alabama 36548

LCCN: 2014950185

ISBN: 978-1-943033-10-2

Chapter 1
Introduction

The objective of this work is to identify true revival, expose false imitations of revival, and to clearly show the difference between the two. Producing a genuine revival in these last days and stirring hearts to find and participate in true revival is the sole reason for this book. ~ **Kenneth G Morris.**

Then

It was stunning and spectacular. It was almost unbelievable, yet it could not be denied. An entire congregation had seen it. It was a miracle. A literal, tangible, visible miracle. It was obvious to all who were in the house. It did not have to be announced or proclaimed. This miracle did not have to be accepted by faith or some stretch of the imagination. It was apparent to the physical sense of sight.

A church in a south Alabama town was the setting. A mother, burdened by the fact her child could not hold its head erect due to underdeveloped muscles in the neck, brought the child forward to be prayed for. Prayer was made. The mother removed her hand from supporting the child's head and the head did not fall to one side as it had been doing, but remained upright. The child, being perhaps three or four years old, could now support its head as a child its age would be expected to do.

~~~

As a small, country congregation praised God, neighbors in the surrounding community saw flames coming from the roof of the little frame church. Doing what good neighbors should, they came to help extinguish the blaze. Upon their arrival they found the building was not on fire at all.

No one could explain it. It was supernatural. A miracle. A sign from God.

It's not hard to imagine the effect these events had on people as they witnessed a divine act of God. No human manipulation, no trickery, no religious mind games, no leader trying to build an ego, just a sovereign act of God. God revealed His power that men might believe on Him.

Now

Contrast these things with a church where the atmosphere is cold and indifferent.

The congregation yawns, and some sleep, as the minister recites poetry or reads a sermon that he did not receive by divine inspiration from God. The crowd has no eye or ear for the spiritual. The eye is on the clock and the ear is waiting to hear the last amen so the people can get out of there and involve themselves in some worldly pleasure or entertainment. Walking through the church door on a Sunday morning fulfills their obligations. They will not be back until next week. In fact, God will be given little thought and even a smaller amount of time from these modern Christians on the six other days of the week.

There are gatherings—and some of them are quite large—where emotions are high and audience participation is enthusiastic. However, even these gatherings are different and fall short of the old time revival meetings in many ways. Motivation, the power behind the emotionalism, is quite different. Loud music, special lighting effects, prominent personalities, trained manipulators, none of these were present in previous times.

Today, people by the tens of thousands gather in a city and with high media exposure go through a highly intense religious exercise, yet leave that city with no lasting impact. Evil and evil men are in no way arrested. Crime and violence continue. This is not the way it should be.

In the first church, one-hundred-twenty people, after a ten day meeting, changed not only the course of a city, but turned the world upside down.

Is there a real, Biblical, New Testament revival in America today?

Sin

Real revival deals with sin first. If there is sin and disease present, disease will be dealt with, but not until sin is first dealt with.

This is the way the prophets of the Old Testament did it. John the Baptist did it this way. Christ, our perfect example, followed this course. Every revival in history adhered to this formula.

It is futile to deal with disease and ignore sin—the cause of the disease.

Christ said to operate in this fashion, would cause a worse thing to come on an individual or a nation. "Go and sin no more" were His words to those blessed in His presence.

Blessings

In real revival, blessings follow commitment and not vice versa. When the attitude, "Lord, if you will bless me, I will serve you," is found, there is no revival in that place. Seeking Christ and His kingdom first, above everything else, is the proper attitude of revival. Those who follow Him looking for His blessing rather than looking for Him are misled and will suffer bitter disappointment in the end.

Prosperity

An increase in material things, is not always a sign of revival. To have one's needs supplied is God's will, but these things are tied directly to the prosperity of the soul in scripture.

Prosperity and wealth can be had through crooked means and ways that are evil. Many of the richest people in the world do not even believe in God. A very large percentage of the world's money is owned and controlled by a group who have denied the deity and the messiahship of Jesus Christ. Yet many believe the false concept that riches and spirituality are synonymous.

To be poor or needy is to be out of step with God is their philosophy. This is not biblical, and nothing could be further from the truth.

A rich man and a beggar lived in the same town. The rich man died and went to hell. The beggar died and was carried by angels into the presence of the Lord. This is proof from the ultimate authority, the Bible, that materialism and prosperity are not gauges whereby spiritual judgments can be made.

Crowds

Church growth and large crowds are not the standard by which we judge revival. Revival many times will produce a crowd but a crowd in and by itself will never produce revival.

If huge gatherings of people constitute revival, then Adolf Hitler should be considered a great revivalist. The abortion rights activists rally in large numbers, but their demonstrations cannot be labeled as having the blessings of the Lord on them.

Many are of the impression that God is with the crowd or multitude. There are times when this is true. Multitudes gathered by the seashore to hear the teachings of Christ and to be blessed by His presence. On occasions He had to escape to the mountain or across the sea from the multitude.

There was also a time when—because of His teachings—the multitude left Him. Perhaps the greatest account of any conversion wrought by Jesus took place at a well with no one present but Himself and one woman.

Offerings

Large amounts of money being brought into the treasury of the church is not a sign of revival. At one point in His ministry, the Lord sent one of His disciples fishing so money could be had for taxes. God's power is not tied to nor limited by the availability of money. "Silver and gold have I none, but such as I have, give I thee," were the words spoken to a lame man just as he was about to be healed. A revival of God's healing power came to this man, and he walked, leapt and praised God in the absence of money.

Manifestations

Emotionalism and sensationalism are the signs of revival many look for. The stirring of the inner emotions of an individual causing a peculiar movement of the body or body parts is the goal of many who minister in the services. Great stock and importance are placed on these manifestations even to the point of satisfaction, although the person or persons being ministered to are not saved, healed, or delivered.

Such expressions as, "he shouted" or "she was slain in the Spirit," are often repeated as proof that the fire of God has fallen, and a great refreshing has come.

It is true that in the midst of a real outpouring of the Spirit, emotions will run high as the emotions are stirred by the spirit, but if emotionalism brought revival or was a sign of revival then the ball stadium would be the place to be.

Sensationalism and psychic phenomenon such as passing out or losing one's sense of place and time are often present where the spirit of God is moving and should be accepted as a genuine mark of blessing. However, these alone cannot be the basis by which we identify revival as long as these same things are happening at rock concerts and in country music halls throughout the land. If someone screaming or passing out is the objective, then many of the world's performers have achieved that objective.

Zeal and Ambition

Zeal and ambition are not signs of an outpouring. Nor can these alone produce the spiritual awakening so desperately needed now. Zeal is good, if it is according to knowledge. An ambitious person can be a real asset to the kingdom of God if the ambition is not a selfish one, and the person is intent on glorifying none but God. A sincere heart can be sincerely wrong as has been witnessed by observing many modem day cults and their leaders. Some have followed these charismatic leaders to the death, being led astray by zeal, ambition, and sincerity.

Truth

As long as the church exists in this world, there will be:
- the real and the unreal
- the true and the untrue
- the genuine and the false
- the working of God
- the workings of Satan.

Revival and a counterfeit of revival will be around until the church is raptured.

Responsibility to know the difference and to embrace the true while rejecting the false rests, with the church. Counterfeits are made to resemble the true article as much as possible for the sake of deception.

It is a simple thing to see clearly the religious counterfeits of the past. History and time have proved them false. Persons and movements that were not of God have come to naught.

The present is a different story. The convenience of knowing the end results of the many and varied movements that confront this generation is not available. History can be read. The future must be experienced. Today's future is tomorrow's past.

Only one opportunity is given to live any one day. No day has ever existed twice. When it is gone, it is gone. The clock of time cannot be turned back. A day lived with deceit is lost forever. Therefore, it is extremely important to know the truth.

Ability to discern the spirits of this world and to be able to execute righteous judgment is not an option. It is a necessity. Narrow mindedness leads to disaster by causing a denial of everything. Broad mindedness leads to trouble by accepting everything that comes along. Both of these will hinder the soul.

The prayer of every person desirous of real revival should be to become broad minded enough to accept truth and narrow minded enough to reject error.

Chapter 2
Ghost of Revivals Past

As soon as it is announced that the altar is open for seekers for pardon, sanctification, the baptism in the Holy Ghost, and healing for the body, people rise and flock to the altar. There is no urging. What kind of preaching is it that brings that? It is the simple declaring of the Word of God. There is such power in the preaching of the Word in the Spirit that people are shaken on the benches. Coming to the altar many fall prostrate under the power of God and often come out speaking in tongues.- <u>With Signs Following</u>, written by Stanley H. Frodsham and published by the Gospel Publishing House (1946) describing the Azusa Street Revival.

The news spread far and wide that Los Angeles was being visited with a rushing mighty wind from Heaven. The how and why of it is found in the very opposite of those conditions that are usually thought necessary for a big revival.

No instruments of music are used. None are needed. No choir. Bands of angels have been heard by some in the Spirit and there is heavenly singing that is inspired by the Holy Ghost. No collections are taken. No bills have been posted to advertise the meetings. No church organization is behind it.

All who are in touch with God realize as soon as they enter the meeting that the Holy Ghost is the leader. One brother states that even before his train entered the city he felt the power of the revival. Travelers from afar wind their way to the headquarters at Azusa Street. There they find a two story, whitewashed store building. You would hardly expect heavenly visitations there unless you remember the stable at Bethlehem. But here they find a mighty Pentecostal revival going on from ten o'clock in the morning until about twelve o'clock at night. Pentecost has come to hundreds of hearts.

Encouragement

In a 1905 letter written to Frank Bartleman—one of the leaders of the Azusa Street revival, Evan Roberts—the most prominent evangelist in the Welsh revival of 1904, wrote, "My dear brother in the faith: many thanks for your kind letter. I am impressed of your sincerity and honesty of purpose. Congregate the people together who are willing to make a total surrender. Pray and wait. Believe God's promises. Hold daily meetings. May God bless you is my earnest prayer."

Again in November of 1905, Evan Roberts wrote to Mr. Bartleman, "My dear comrade: What can I say that will encourage you in this terrible fight. I find it is a most awful one. The kingdom of the evil one is being besieged on every side. Oh, the millions of prayers, not simply the form of prayer, but the soul finding its way right to the White Throne! May the Lord bless you with a mighty down pouring. We had a mighty down pouring of the Holy Spirit last Saturday night. This was preceded by the correcting of the people's views of true worship. 1.-To give unto God, not to receive. 2.-To please God and not ourselves. Therefore, looking to God, and forgetting the enemy, and also the fear of men, we prayed, and the Spirit descended. I pray God to hear your prayer, to keep your faith strong, and save California. I remain your brother in the fight."

Looking back on these and other awakenings of the past should give insight into what it takes to produce revival. Those seeking the latter rain would do well to examine the actions of those who were recipients of the early rain beginning with those in the Upper Room at Pentecost and continuing down through the history of the church.

The latter rain must come from the same source as the early rain. That source being God our Father. The latter rain must be the same as the early rain. This being the Holy Ghost. The result of the latter rain must be the same as the result of the early rain. That result being precious fruit of the earth being presented to the husbandman. That husbandman being Jesus Christ.

The same source, the same rain, the same result demands that the same basic course of action be taken to receive the latter rain.

Unique Vessels

A study of past revivals reveals significant differences. These differences occur mainly because of personalities, localities, and social conditions. However, revivals of all ages have much in common. These similarities are the foundation and basis of true revival. Without them, there is no revival then or now.

Differences of methods and administration are to be expected. John Wesley's methods differed from those of Charles Finney, yet both experienced revival because both had a basic knowledge of the requirements to see God move in their lives and in their ministries.

Jonathan Edward's style of preaching was totally different from that of George Whitfield's. Yet both knew if cities, towns, and communities were to be affected, in a positive way, God's Word must be proclaimed without compromise or apology.

Therefore it is not Wesley's methods or Finney's administration that should be studied for the sake of imitation. Impersonating Edwards or preaching like Whitfield will avail absolutely nothing. It is their motives, their resolves, their burdens, their prayers, their attitudes toward sin and sinful men, their concept of God and His Word, their dedication to truth, their fearlessness and courage, that must be echoed in lives and ministries if similar results are to be duplicated today.

Through study and practice, the ability to preach or perform as another can be achieved. But unless the private prayer life and personal dedication and devotion of the other is also emulated nothing positive will be accomplished. It is foolish to think that copying styles will bring results. God does not bless styles. He blesses obedience, honesty and sincerity. For this reason God blesses individuals who are vastly different in mannerisms and dispositions. Some have witnessed remarkable results ministering to the sick in a gentle and easy manner while some who were reckless, even to the point of physically hitting or slapping the afflicted, were equally successful.

Many are the accounts of miracles being wrought as the

great Apostle of Faith, Smith Wigglesworth, would make a fist and strike someone in the stomach or push and shove a cripple while commanding that person to walk or run. One gentle, one rough, but the results are the same. How can this be? It can only be concluded that God is honoring something other than style. So since it is not styles and mannerisms that are being blessed, then it is useless to copy them.

Samson used a jawbone of an ass on one occasion to win a great victory. It is common knowledge to all who study scripture that the power did not lie within the jawbone. The power was in being obedient to the Nazarite Vow. As long as that obedience was maintained the choice of weapon or method was of secondary importance. When that vow was violated then no weapon or method would avail.

A smooth stone from a brook did not make a giant killer out of David. It was David's faith, which could not be shaken, that brought Goliath to the ground. So what is the truth here? It is a simple truth. Five stones from a brook will not make a giant killer of an individual who has a faith that wavers.

These truths being evident, an examination of principles and foundations of past revivals should serve well a generation in need of and who are seeking revival for their present time. More time is spent studying the **personalities** of the past rather than studying the **principles** of the past. God uses people in His work. This is clearly disclosed in the statement, "The sword of the Lord and of Gideon". (Judges 7:18) However, it is not the person but things about the person that are to be credited for the work being done.

The Welsh Revival and the Azusa Street Revival are examples of this truth. If God had been looking for personalities to use in the revival in Wales in 1904, and the Azusa Street outpouring in Los Angeles in 1906, He would have chosen them from the popular clergy. There were men alive in that era, whose names, history has recorded as being among the very best speakers, orators and authors. Instead, in the little country of Wales, a twenty-six year old coal miner emerged as the proclaimed leader while in Los Angeles the acknowledged leader of the Azusa Street mission was a little known black man who was handicapped by blindness in one eye.

By choosing to use men from lower levels of social status, God sent a clear message to all. It is:
- principle not personality
- the Creator not the created
- Holy Ghost power not programs
- praying not playing
- fasting not feasting
- interceding not entertaining
- purity not popularity.

When these facts, which are proven by history, are grasped and applied, the result will always be an outpouring of the Spirit of God in revival. The fire will fall.

"It is not by might nor by power but by my spirit," saith the Lord. Zachariah 4:6

Mentoring

Some of these principles of revival can be found in the letters written by Evan Roberts referred to earlier in this chapter. Christians in Los Angeles were seeking a supernatural visitation from God. So sincere was this desire that one of them, Frank Bartleman, wrote to Evan Roberts on at least three occasions. The purpose of this correspondence was twofold: first, to ask prayer of the Christians in Wales, and second, to be instructed in the ways of revival.

Guidance came from the man of God in this fashion. Only individuals who were willing to make a total surrender to God and the cause of revival were to be dealt with. No one else need apply. These were to hold daily meetings. The purpose of these meetings being to pray, wait, and believe God's promises. Mr. Bartleman's mind was also reinforced in a most important truth. He was engaged in warfare. "What can I say to encourage you in this terrible fight? I find it is a most awful one," were the words of Evan Roberts. True worship was also described in this correspondence. The believer must learn "To give unto God, not receive." and "To please God and not ourselves."

These admonitions did not come from the pen of a religious practitioner content with a form of Godliness. There was no guess work, no question or uncertainty in these instructions. Phrases such as, these things might work or perhaps these suggestions will help, were never used nor implied.

These guidelines for revival came from the pen of one of the most anointed men in recent history. From the very fires of revival they came. These were tried principles and proven methods. They had worked in Wales. Would they not also work across the ocean, in another environment, and on another continent? Would differing dialects and cultures demand differing principles or rules of revival? Did the applications of these religious principles prove successful in America? Of course, the answers to these questions are found to be positive as a backward look is made to the Azusa Street Mission. Not only did revival come to California, it spread across the entire nation. The eyewitness account that opened this chapter stated, "The news spread far and wide that Los Angeles was being visited with a rushing mighty wind from heaven."

An analysis of this report reveals many enlightening facts pertaining to revival. Credit is given to the "Rushing mighty Wind" not to a person or group of persons.

Many things thought essential today were not present then:

Music

There were no musical instruments of any kind. To employ instruments of music in religious meetings is not wrong, for the scripture alludes to the use of them. However, this proves that they are not necessary for the spirit to move.

Music can and should complement revival, but music can never produce revival.

Emotions are aroused by music. This is true in the secular sense, as well as, the spiritual. Night halls of worldly pleasure and amusement could not exist without music. Emotionalism produced by the playing of music—that exist as long as the music beat goes on—is not to be equated with the fire of God. If the moving of the spirit stops when the music stops, then the wrong spirit is moving. A crowd does not have to be sensitized with rhythm or beat for there to be a visitation of the Almighty. History proves this. It happened at Azusa.

Money

No collections were taken. What would a crusade be today without buckets from the local fried chicken restaurant being passed before the congregation? Let no mistake be made, scripture, and especially the book of Acts, teaches the principle of giving to the work of God. In today's economy, money is available and it is essential, but never let it be said that the amount of money coming into the coffers in any way determine the availability of the power of God.

Supernatural things can neither be bought nor sold. When this was tried by Simon the sorcerer, the apostle Peter said to him, "'Thy money perish with these because thou hast thought that the gift of God may be purchased with money."

When more time is taken with the collection than in dealing with the sick, suffering, bound, and lost, revival has not come to that place.

Advertisement

People traveled from many countries of the world to a little mission on Azusa Street to hear the Word, to witness the miraculous, and to be filled with the Spirit. They heard, saw and were blessed.

Returning to their own places, they helped spread the fire.

From this humble place many parts of the world were touched by the message of Pentecost. It was nothing less than phenomenal. Yet all of this transpired in the absence of any form of formal advertisement. The account given earlier stated, "No bills have been posted to advertise the meetings." No advertisement was needed. The Holy Ghost advertised Himself to Jerusalem on the day of Pentecost. "Now when this was noised abroad, the multitude came together." Acts 2:6

Some things can be kept quiet and hidden, but the falling of the fire of God is not one of them.

Prompting

It is also evident from this eye witness account of the revival of 1906, that no mind manipulating through hypnosis or psychology was needed to bring men and women to a decision. As soon as the altars were opened they were filled with seekers. "There is no urging," so states our witness. Individuals must be drawn by the Spirit. "No man can come to me, except the Father which hath sent me draw him." John 6:44

Coming to Christ is a thing of the spirit and not of the mind.

A look at past revivals should be an inspiration and encouragement to this present generation. Many have given up all hope of a spiritual awakening. Contentment with the status quo seems to be the prevailing attitude.

May the knowledge of these great outpourings, obtained from a careful study of history, haunt the minds and spirits of a sleeping church world—a church that needs nothing so far as material wealth is concerned, a church well trained and well equipped.

Let the congregation meeting in a marvel of architectural beauty be haunted by the memory of a group who, less than a century ago, met in an old discarded building that had at one time been used as a Methodist church but had been vacant for years.

The recollection of a twenty-six year old coal miner who received a call from God and obeyed that call to such an extent that his entire nation felt the shaking of God's power, should haunt modem preachers as they lie on their beds of comfort.

Church members sleeping on pews, padded for comfort, should be haunted by the memory of the faithful, sitting on homemade benches constructed of rough lumber, straining to hear the Word of God.

That generation walked to the meeting place or rode a wagon or some other crude method of transportation. This generation rides to church in fine, air-conditioned automobiles.

If the memory of the past does not inspire and encourage this generation into action, and if the spirits of men and women of the past do not haunt men and women of today, prodding them into action, then what will the outcome be? The answer is simple. A generation will be lost, and the Ghost of revivals past will be the witnesses that stands against it in the great Day of Judgment.

Chapter 3
Fervent Praying

"More things are wrought by prayer than the world dreams of." ~ **Tennyson**

"Unless I had the spirit of prayer, I could do nothing. If even for a day or an hour I lost the spirit of grace and supplication, I found myself unable to preach with power and efficiency, or to win souls by personal conversation." These words came from the heart of the man some have called the greatest revivalist of all times, Charles G. Finney.

Revival for Charles Finney was an impossibility aside from prayer—fervent prayer. The relationship between prayer and revival has been realized by men and women of every age who obtained a visitation of God.

The present class of religious leaders must also come to terms with this reality:

- No prayer means no power.
- No travail equals no triumph.
- No gaining where there is no groaning.
- No conversation with heaven translates into no converts in the church.
- The absence of supplication is accompanied by

the absence of supernatural visitation.
- Neither thinking, hoping, wishing, nor positive confession will substitute for prayer.

"The effectual, fervent prayer of a righteous man availeth much." James 5:16

Allowing the fire to go out on the altar was one of Israel's greatest mistakes. Preceding the loss of the Ark of the Covenant, these words are recorded, "Ere the lamp of God went out in the temple of the Lord, where the Ark of God was." I Samuel 3:3

The religious climate is always directly tied to the climate of the prayer closets. When prayer closets and prayer rooms are heated by the fervent prays of the saints, the sanctuary is heated by the falling of heavenly fire. Coldness in the arena of prayer means coldness in the arena of ministry. Ashes on a dry and dusty altar choke and strangle the breath of God.

Many altars that were once ablaze with the glowing flames of heaven rending prayer now hold only ashes, grim reminders of the days when soul saving power was alive in the midst. Only a return to real praying will bring real revival. Heaven is silent toward the church when the church is silent toward heaven. When heaven hears from the church, then and only then, will the church hear from heaven. When the prayer bells of heaven ring through the streets of the celestial city, then the shouts of victory and glory will ring through the streets of our cities and towns as the fire falls once again. The sounds of weeping must be heard "between the porch and the altar." Joel 2:17

Ghost of Revivals Past

Many great outpourings of the spirit have been immortalized through historical records. By examining these records it is discovered, without fail or exception, that the key was prayer. Personalities, locations, time frames, social conditions and many other things were factors but prayer was the key. The correspondence from Evan Roberts to Frank Bartleman—referred to in the previous chapter—made reference to the "millions of prayers, not simply the form of prayer, but the soul finding its way right to the 'White Throne." It is easy to see from the pen of the most visible person who had a part in the revival in Wales in 1904, that the single most important ingredient of that awakening was, "the millions of prayers" Not tens, not hundreds, not thousands but millions of prayers! A generation that merely claims it or confesses it by faith but never prays for it fervently, will never see it.

Much has been made of the fact that the Azusa Revival happened in an abandoned building, which some say was once used as a stable. This should surprise no one, seeing that Christ was born in a stable. But it was not the building. It was prayer. Much praying preceded the Los Angeles visitation and there was much praying during the visitation. Frank Bartleman states in his account, "Brother Seymour generally sat behind two empty shoe boxes, one on top of the other. He usually kept his head inside the top one during the meeting in prayer". Contrasting this posture with the posture of some leaders of this time who have a great desire to be seen and heard, sheds some light on the reason for the prevailing spiritual climate of the age.

The names of many great preachers have been preserved for all time by means of the printed page. Men famous for their oratory ability. Famous for great campaigns conducted or great churches established. Names such as Charles G. Finney, D. L. Moody, Smith Wigglesworth, and a host of others. Granted these men were great preachers and great revivalists. These are the things they are remembered for. In the next chapter their preaching will be discussed for it played a definite part in their success. However, it was their praying and communing with God that made them great preachers.

When satisfactory results were not forthcoming in Finney's revivals, he would spend his days in fasting and prayer. Unlike so many today who advocate something other than fervent, extended prayers, this man of God fully believed nothing could be accomplished in revival meetings aside from prayer.

After delivering a very strong sermon that angered the congregation, Finney and a Baptist brother agreed to spend the next day in fasting and prayer. They prayed separately in the morning but united in prayer in the afternoon. As these men of God fasted and prayed the townsfolk were discussing the sermon of the night before with such indignation and animosity that the possibility of tarring and feathering Mr. Finney was raised. Of the prayer meeting Finney stated, "Just at evening the Lord gave us great enlargement and promises of victory. Both of us felt assured that we had prevailed with God; and that the power of God would be revealed among the people."

When time came for the service that evening, the meeting house was packed. Did some come to watch the spectacle? Would the preacher be tarred and feathered? Some came, no doubt, with the same attitude that would have accompanied them to the circus. Thinking this would be the last night of the meeting as the preacher would be driven out of town, they were hardly prepared for a powerful sermon from the text, "say ye to the righteous that it shall be well with him, woe to the wicked! It shall be ill with him." Finney gave this description, 'The Spirit of God came upon me with such power that it was like opening a battery upon them.... The word of God come through me in a manner I could see was carrying all before it. It was a fire and a hammer breaking the rock."

The effects were stunning. One woman fell under the power of the spirit. Throughout the night one after another sent for the evangelist to come and pray for them, but he had gone to another place for the night and could not be found.

One of the opposers of the revival took sick and being told by the doctor that he was dying said, "Don't let Finney pray over my corpse." Finney confirmed this to be the last of the opposition in the place.

In another meeting, a man came armed, intending to kill the man of God, but instead fell from his seat screaming, "I am sinking to hell," as Finney preached.

The results of this revival were nothing less than miraculous. And it happened through prayer.

It was fervent praying that broke the spirit of Satan that held the people of that place in bondage. Had Charles G. Finney been one with a carefree attitude or had he been indoctrinated with the "word of faith" teaching that excludes intense supplication before God and discounts "praying through," he would not have had revival in that place.

He did speak the word of faith. He did claim victory. He did dominate the evil spirit of that town. The authority with which he spoke, the faith through which he claimed victory and the power by which he dominated were all received by him as he prayed. "This kind goeth not out but by prayer and fasting." Matthew 17:21

It is no wonder Finney's preaching was with such awesome power. Frank Bartleman declared that Finney, "forged his theology on the anvil of prayer, in his own heart."

God also added to the ministry of this great man a prayer partner. Not a financial partner, mind you, but a prayer partner. Not a public relations specialist but a prayer partner. Not a spin doctor to polish his image but a prayer partner. This partner was a man called Father Nash.

When Nash, also a minister, was stricken with a disease of the eyes, he gave himself wholly to prayer. Father Nash kept a "praying list"—as he called it—of the names of persons he prayed for every day.

"And praying with him, and hearing him pray in meetings, I found that his gift of prayer was wonderful and his faith almost miraculous," declared Finney of Father Nash.

Many times as these men of God labored together through the years, Father Nash would not attend the meetings. As Finney was preaching, Nash would seclude himself in prayer asking for an outpouring of the spirit. This combination brought revival then, and it will bring revival now. Preaching alone won't do it. "The letter killeth." Preaching and praying will cause Holy Ghost fire to fall. 'Watch and pray" is Christ instructions to the church. 'Watching and playing," will not suffice even when the games are religious ones. Many are playing the tongues game. Some are playing the word of knowledge game. Still others are toying with prophecy. Sing it down, shout it down, is the favorite gimmick of many. War games played by children never trained for war, are vastly different from actual combat. So it is with the church. Revival games—some play them to perfection—never produce revival results. Wars are won and lost, not on the battlefield, but in boot camp. To bypass boot camp and go straight to the trenches is defeat guaranteed. The prayer closet is boot camp for the church. Where there is no sound of pounding feet on the training grounds, there will be the sound of retreating feet on the battleground.

Not only did Finney pray, he so instilled the necessity of prayer into the souls of his hearers, that many after being converted themselves, would spend entire nights praying for others to be saved.

This concept of laity praying—some think that only the ministry should pray—became a crucial factor and a driving force in the life and ministry of a converted shoe salesman from Chicago. D. L. Moody, numbered among the greatest preachers of all times, learned the value of praying lay persons.

Observing the two ladies in the front row seats, it was not hard for Moody to tell they were praying for him. "Why don't you pray for the people?" was Moody's reply to them at the end of the service. "Because you need the power of the spirit," was their reply. Telling this story years later, Moody confessed to having thought; "I need power? Why, I thought I had power. I had the largest church in Chicago and there were many conversions. I was in a sense satisfied."

These ladies kept right on praying until this Godly man's heart was filled with a great hunger.

- Hunger causes men to seek.
- Seeking causes men to find.
- Finding leads to filling.
- Filling brings power.

- Power moves to action and power filled action produces dramatic results.

Who does not know of Moody's great campaign in England in June 1872? Four hundred were converted in a ten day meeting that had not been planned.

D. L. Moody went to London, not intending to preach. Being prevailed upon by the pastor of a North London church, he agreed to preach on a Sunday. The morning service seemed cold, dead, and lifeless. The evening service was the opposite. The Spirit of God came. A hush fell over the congregation. Moody was puzzled at the change. Most of the audience responded when the question "who would like to become a Christian?" was put to them. Amazed, Moody gave instructions to meet with the pastor on Monday night if they were in earnest about this matter. In the Monday evening meeting, these returned and more with them. Mr. Moody left London but on Tuesday was urged to return to the city and the Church. This he did and the results were ten days of glorious revival.

It was sometime later before Moody learned the secret of this outpouring. A bedridden woman, a member of the North London church that experienced the falling of Holy Ghost fire, had read of the great preacher, D. L Moody in the newspapers. This invalid lady began to pray, asking God to send him to her church. Upon learning from her sister that Moody had preached in their church on Sunday morning, she spent the afternoon fasting and praying for the evening service. This explained the difference in the evening meeting.

This great crusade was not the result of diligent planning by an evangelistic committee. There had been none. There was no prior advertisement or promotion. The name or charisma of the evangelist was not responsible for it. It was the prayers of an invalid, bedridden woman. The evangelist was unaware of her efforts but God heard her supplication and answered in a glorious manner. "Pray to thy Father which is in secret: and thy Father which seeth in secret shall reward thee openly." Matthew 6:6

Moody was so dependent on prayer—both his and others—that at one of his Hippodrome meetings in New York, he asked for one thousand Christians to leave the service, go into another building and pray for the meeting. This would allow one thousand of those on the outside to come in and hear the gospel. God's great men and women are men and women of prayer.

Smith Wigglesworth—known as the Apostle of Faith—a man whose ministry many would desire to duplicate, said on occasions that he never prayed for more than thirty minutes at a time. Then he would finish that statement by declaring that he never went longer than thirty minutes without praying. His was constant. His mind was "stayed on the Lord." Wigglesworth also took communion every day. Miracles were not exceptions for this man of prayer and communion. They were common results of his ministry.

How did the church become side tracked from the truth, thinking prayer and supplication could be replaced by a word of faith or some positive confession?

Only through prayer does an individual arrive at the level that enables him or her to speak words of faith and power. "From the abundance of the heart the mouth speaketh." No positive confession, word of faith, or any such thing can come from the lips of any person who does not possess a heart of faith. The heart must have faith before the mouth can speak it. Many are doing a lot of vain talking and spiritual babbling with minimal results, and the lack of prayer is the reason. Necessary heart-faith will not come to the prayerless.

Christ is our example of speaking the word of faith. "Thy faith hath made thee whole," He said to the woman with the issue of Blood. "Thy brother shall live again," was a positive confession to Mary and Martha at the tomb of their brother, Lazarus. The many seasons of prayer, some of them lasting all night, qualified Christ to speak words of faith and to make positive confessions.

Elijah could send a message to Ahab informing him that it would not rain until he said it would, because Elijah, being "a man subject to like passions as we are...prayed earnestly that it might not rain." The prophet prayed it into his heart then prophesied it with his mouth. This same prophet prayed for fire on Mount Carmel and got it. After praying seven times for rain, he then sent Ahab word to prepare his chariot and get home, "that the rain stop thee not."

"Faith without works is dead." Fervent praying is work. Without it, faith is dead and dead faith produces nothing but more death.

Dead preachers are preaching dead sermons to dead people in dead churches. All because the prayer closets are still and lifeless.

It's time to pray.

Chapter 4
Revival Preaching

"A timid tongue and a tender knee never will revival see." ~ Kenneth G. Morris

Meetings and crusades are often labeled as revival when, in reality, they are nothing more than gatherings for the religious crowd.

It is not the meeting place, the attendance or the speaker that qualifies a meeting to be called a revival. It is the results. Whether a gathering of any kind is a revival cannot be ascertained until said gathering is over or at least has been in progress for a period of time. Faith, hope and trust prompt meetings to be announced beforehand as revival, but many times the fire does not fall, revival does not come. The results prove this to be so.

There are many individual results of revival. However, these individual results occur because of two things:
- a renewal of religious experience
- a return to and a recovery of spiritual truths.

In this day of pseudo-revival, it is the renewal of religious experiences that is sought after. "Truth is fallen in the streets," Isaiah 59:14 and there are but few who seek to recover it.

Many covet the signs, wonders, miracles and blessings while ignoring the truth. This is evident as those who are supposedly slain in the spirit, receive a word of knowledge or prophecy, or have some other spiritual experience, leave the meeting and continue to live a life style of sin contrary to the truth of God's word.

The liar can see, hear and feel great and marvelous sights and sounds but has not experienced revival as long as the lying continues. The fire has not fallen on the thief, no matter the extent of experience, so long as the fingers are "sticky."

The recovery of truth is the missing element in today's religious climate. Experiences abound, but without the recovery of truth to go with these experiences there can be no revival. A dollar's worth of groceries cannot be purchased with a fifty-cent piece. It is only half enough.

Revival preaching is preaching that reintroduces these truths. Healers and prophets are wonderful. Many desire these ministries and rightly so, but where are the preachers? Preachers that will preach in such a way as to bring back truth, Bible truth, are necessary to revival. They are almost as scarce as they are necessary.

The world has an abundant supply of professional preachers, but revival preaching preachers are not so readily available. Men and women whose goal is revival will lead men into "all truth." Softness, vagueness and illusiveness in the pulpit will never spawn revival. Revival preaching says what it means and means what it says. Billy Sunday, the great evangelist whose ministry resulted in approximately one million souls won to Christ, had this to say, "Revival preaching never leaves people wondering where they stand or of the spiritual state of the hearer."

All true revivalists display some basic characteristics:
- humility
- fearlessness
- boldness
- vividness
- compassion.

They minister with a purpose. They do not just mark time or take stabs in the dark. Their purpose is to reveal relevant truth in a plain, simple way so as to bring people to the point of decision.

The proud and arrogant, those with a peacock syndrome, should never expect to see real spiritual awakening. The need is for humanity to see Jesus not some high society, egotistical reverend. Instead of the sweet toned voice of a trained orator, the world must hear the voice of God.

In Scotland a young minister, less than thirty years of age, grasped this truth and witnessed in seven and one-half years of his short ministry a mighty revival in the city of Dundee.

Writing to his friend William Chalmers Bums, also a great revivalist, Robert Murry McCheyne had this to say, "Moses wist not that the skin of his face shone. Looking at our own shining face is the bane of the spiritual life and of the ministry. Oh, for closest communion with God so soul and body shine with divine brilliancy, but oh, for a holy ignorance of our shining!"

"Ministers," McCheyene told an audience, "are but the pole. It is to the brazen serpent you must look." It was no coincidence that revival came to Dundee, Scotland. God found a humble servant to work through.

If money and prestige were taken away many would quit

the ministry. This is true of the professional preacher but it is not so with the revivalist who has a purpose. Their goal is not a pat on the back or padding in the wallet. The desire of these men and women is to be a catalyst of revival; the spark used to ignite the fire.

"One spark can do more to prove the power of powder than a whole library written on the subject." ~ Billy Sunday

Fire in the bosom is worth more than a title before or a degree after the name. A burden for the lost is of more value than theological training.

Individuals finding salvation is the goal of the true revivalist. Cost nor consequence can change that goal. It cannot be compromised. It is the force that drives. Everything else gives in to that intent.

T. DeWitt Talmage, that great preacher of the Nineteenth Century who witnessed as many as six thousand conversions in a single year, had strong thoughts and words on this subject. "We spend three years in college studying ancient mythology and three years in the theological seminary learning how to make a sermon, and then we go out to save the world, and if we cannot do it according to Claude's Sermonizing or Blair's Rhetoric or Kane's Criticism, we will let the world go to Perdition. If we save nothing else we will save Claude and Blair. The work of the religious teacher is to save men; and though every law of grammar should be snapped in the undertaking, and there be nothing but awkwardness and blundering in the mode, all hail to the man who saves a soul from death."

This was the thing that brought such phenomenal success to the ministry of Billy Sunday. Hear it from his own words. "You will agree with me, I am not a crank. At least I try not to be. I have not preached about my first, second, third or hundredth blessing. I have not talked about baptism or immersion. I told you that while I was here my creed would be; with Christ you are saved; without him you are lost. Are you saved? Are you lost? Going to Heaven or going to Hell? I have tried to build every sermon right around these questions and to steer around anything else."

There is no need to search any further for the reason so many walked the "sawdust trail."

Fearfulness and timidness flees from the person with a burden for the lost. Where there is an obsession for revival, there will be a boldness. The prize makes the battle worthwhile.

Fear marks a preacher as one not having a burden for the lost. Many know the truth, but refuse to proclaim it. They are afraid:

- of the faces in the pew
- positions could be lost
- reputations could be ruined
- some member might leave
- the dollar total might decrease
- the possibility of an uprising among the flock.

The shepherd is afraid of the sheep. He no longer leads the flock into green pastures. No longer does he take them to still waters. When the shepherd becomes afraid of the sheep, he should look for another line of work. Revival will never come into such situations.

Those blessed by God in the past to see revival have been those who were "not afraid of their faces."

- They were bold as lions and as fearless as serpents.

- They angered people, stirring their emotions.
- They were extremely controversial.
- They suffered.
- They were threatened.

One, James McReady, had his life threatened in a letter written in blood. They gave their best efforts to see revival, and see revival they did.

This boldness was born out of a love for the truth. Knowing revival cannot exist aside from the truth, they were not afraid to speak it.

Billy Sunday declared, "I believe the Bible is the Word of God from cover to cover. I believe that the man who magnifies the Word of God in his preaching is the man God will honor."

Why do names such as Wesley, Whitefield, Finney, and Luther loom large on the pages of history? Because of their fearless denunciation of all sin, and because they preached Jesus Christ without fear or favor.

Billy Sunday talked about the courage of Wesley, Whitefield, Finney and Luther, yet he came behind none of them in this department.

In his search for revival and his preaching for souls, he said, "But somebody says a revival is abnormal. You lie! Do you mean to tell me that the godless, card playing conditions of the church are normal? I say they are not. It is the abnormal state. It is the sin-eaten, apathetic condition of the church that is abnormal. It is the Dutch lunch and beer party, card parties and the like, that are abnormal. What we need is the old time kind of revival that will make you love your neighbor and quit talking about them. A revival that will make you pay your debts and have family prayers."

Again Mr. Sunday proclaimed, "There are too many Sunday school teachers who are godless card-players, beer, wine and champagne drinkers. No wonder the kids are going to the devil. No wonder your children grow up like cattle when you have no prayer in the home."

Hard, harsh and insensitive are but some of the words this modern generation would use to describe this kind of preaching. A frown and a scowl are expressions that the present church, in its cold state, would give to this bold preaching. Cowardly preachers, who don't know the meaning of the word revival, would denounce such expounding today as being crude and inappropriate.

Yet God smiled on it and blessed it.

Compromisers and soft peddlers must of necessity turn their churches into billiard parlors and recreational rooms to draw a crowd. Membership standards must be lowered or removed to accommodate the worldly minded. Service schedules are conveniently arranged so as not to interfere with the Super Bowl or some other activity.

It is not so with those who fear nothing but God and seek nothing but God's will and the souls of men. Listening to a sermon will reveal at least two things about any preacher:

1. who he fears
2. what his goals are.

"The fear of the Lord is the beginning of knowledge," Proverbs 1:7 and "he that winneth souls is wise." Proverbs 11:30

Boldness to declare the truth of God's Word and courage to warn the wicked of his ways, are foundations on which God can build. Nothing lasting can be built on the teaching and preaching of the fearful and faint hearted. Their stand and standard changes with every change in society or every time a new tithing member comes into the church. Like tumbleweeds in the desert they are driven with the wind. Being driven by the winds of this world guarantees the deadness of that preacher and his crowd.

Jesus Christ the same yesterday, and to day, and for ever, the constant, the unchanging Word is the only foundation on which the Holy Ghost will build. All else is sand.

The story of one whose ministry was in full swing at the end of the nineteenth century and the beginning of the twentieth century illustrates well the fact that bold and fearless preaching brings positive result. John Alexander Dowie was born in Edinburgh, Scotland, May 25, 1847. He immigrated to Australia with his parents at the age of thirteen. In the year 1874, a terrible plague swept through the countryside where Dowie was laboring as pastor.

In just a few weeks this young man had officiated at more than forty funerals. In a state of deep sorrow the truth of Christ the Healer was revealed to him. The popular opinion that the plague was from the Lord was driven from Dowie as Acts 10:38 was illuminated to his mind.

The sorrowing pastor now understood that Satan was the defiler and Christ was the Healer. Armed with this fresh knowledge of truth, this man of God bucked the tide of popular feeling and began to proclaim the message of divine healing. The ministry of divine healing will not work in the absence of holy living. Thus of necessity holy living, through separation from the sins of the world, became an integral part of Dowie's message.

In the year 1888, Dowie arrived in America, finally settling in Chicago. In that great midwestern city, wonderful things began to happen as the bold and fearless message of God was proclaimed.

- God blessed.
- Souls were won.
- Bodies were healed.
- A great church was established and soon thousands were attending.

Chicago's reputation as a city where booze flowed almost as freely as water in the sewer, was well established. It did not take long for the preacher from Australia to be made aware of the prominence of the alcohol traffic. Being informed of the matter, it was not long before his attack of this ungodly evil began with a righteous zeal and a holy vengeance. Undaunted by opposition and persecution, Dowie was arrested one hundred times in the year 1895 alone. He boldly proclaimed truth.

"When Christ comes into a house," Dowie thundered. "The devil has to get out, and when Christ comes into your spirit, the devil has to get out of your spirit. If you are going to receive Jesus Christ by faith, then you must understand the terms on which He will come. He will come on the condition that you will do what He tells you, even in your eating and drinking. Then you won't drink whiskey, you won't drink beer, you won't drink brandy or gin, or any other of the liquid fire and distilled damnation that is made and sold under ordinance in this city, and that men drink to their damnations here and hereafter; the champagne, which is a sham at night and a pain in the morning. You won't drink poisons for they defile."

The message to the dead, formal religious crowd was no softer. With no fear of the religious crowd Dowie stated, "You say that you are an average Christian. Well, what is that?

'Well, I get shaved every Sunday morning, and put on my best clothes and go to church.'

Well, what more?

'I join in a little in the singing, I like music very much, and I sit back and listen to the choir.'

Well, what else?

'I pay for the singers and the preacher, of course. We have a smart up-to-date parson. Oh, he does preach wonderfully! He never hurts anybody; he never calls anybody names as you do; he says we are mighty good people and pats us on the back, and he is a smart fellow. Yes siree, I am no saint, I am an average Christian.'

Well, my friend, you are very candid, and I will be the same. I will tell you what you are. You are a sham and a fraud. If all your Christianity lies in helping to pay a quartet and a minister to read and say nice things for you, and then go back to the stock exchange and your various other pursuits to act in the same ungodly way as before, you are a sham and a liar, and it is my duty as God's minister to tell you so."

Horrible and insensitive! Cruel and outrageous! Are the public reactions to such preaching, but how does Heaven react to bold, fearless exhortations? There are records available to answer this question.

- Sadie Cody, niece of Colonel W.F. "Buffalo Bill" Cody, traveled from Rensselaer, Indiana on a cot to Dowie's place in Chicago. Suffering from a diseased spine, abscess, tumor, internal disorders, and her right leg three inches shorter than the left, she was ministered to. Four months later Sadie Cody witnessed to the healing power of God. She was made whole.

- President Abraham Lincoln's cousin, Miss Amanda M. Hicks, of Clinton, Kentucky, was healed through Dowie's ministry.
- *There's Honey In The Rock* is a blessed hymn of the church. Its author, Rev. F.A. Graves, was also healed through the prayers of this man of God.
- Mr. Dowie's church grew rapidly until by the year 1900 the number of adherents numbered in the tens of thousands.
- Zion, a city located north of Chicago on Lake Michigan which thrives to this day, was founded by Dowie in 1901 as a place for Christians to live, work and worship.

Although in his later years, John Alexander Dowie did some things that were foolish and wrong, his ministry is proof that God uses the bold and fearless to restore truth to the church.

On the rugged Kentucky frontier, great camp meeting fires blazed as men like Peter Cartwright defended the gospel. After having rebuked a woman calling her "an old hypocritical, lying woman," Cartwright was approached by a mad husband. "Sir, this is my wife, and I will defend her at the risk of my life," was the husband's words. To this, Peter Cartwright replied, "This is my camp meeting, and I will maintain the good order of it at the risk of my life. If this is your wife, take her off from here, and clear yourselves in five minutes, or I will have you under guard."

Truth must be restored before revival will come. It cannot be restored by the faint of heart. "Be not afraid of their faces: for I am with thee," Jeremiah 1:8.

Chapter 5
Simple Preaching

**"I want to preach the gospel so plainly that men can come from the factories and not have to bring a dictionary!"
~ Billy Sunday.**

This statement by the great revivalist reveals yet another reason for his tremendous success in the business of winning souls to Christ.

Revival preaching is simple preaching.

Salvation, obtained by simple faith in Christ, is placed beyond the reach of many; and others are made to not want it, because some pulpiteer has to show off a new word he has learned.

The congregation sat in wondering silence as the preacher announced from the pulpit that the glory of the Lord could be seen on each physiognomy. It was a welcomed relief to many after an explanation for those who might not know, that he was speaking of their faces.

This type of self-show has no place in revival preaching. Christ himself—one who possessed all knowledge—would never have spoken in such a manner. His only goal was to "do the will of the Father," and bring salvation to mankind.

T. DeWitt Talmage said of Christ, "He upset all their notions as to how preaching ought to be done. There was this peculiarity about His preaching, the people knew what He meant. His illustrations were taken from the hen calling her chicks together, from salt, from candles, from fishing tackle, from a hard creditor collaring a debtor. The common people heard Him gladly."

It is not what the preacher knows, but who the preacher knows, that will bring revival. God never puts a premium on ignorance. Neither does He make education a qualification for ministry. Although ministers come from every point of the literate compass, some educated to the highest degree possible, while others are illiterate, the Word has all to know, "It's not by might nor by power but by my Spirit says the Lord."

Billy Sunday said, "I don't know any more about theology than a jack rabbit knows about ping pong, but I'm on my way to glory."

He knew "Jesus Christ and Him crucified." He knew the saving grace of God. He knew he was saved. He knew it was God's will to save others. Billy Sunday knew that Jesus was the same today as before.

- What Christ was, He still is.
- What He did, He still does.

Mr. Sunday knew there is a Heaven and that the saved would go there and that there is a hell and the lost go there. This was all he needed to know and all he needed to preach. God blessed the simple message of the former ball player, Billy Sunday.

The same can be said of John Wesley. Though educated to the highest degree, and trained to the fullest in theology, he realized the importance of the simple gospel message in his quest for great things from God.

"I desire plain truth for plain people," proclaimed Wesley. "Therefore, of set purpose, I abstain from all nice and philosophical speculations, from all perplexed and intricate reasonings, and as far as possible, from even the show of learning, unless in sometimes citing the original Scripture. I labor to avoid all words which are not easy to be understood, all which are not used in common life and, in particular, those kinds of technical terms that so frequently occur in bodies of divinity, those modes of speaking which men of reading are intimately acquainted with, but which, to common people are an unknown tongue."

Had John Wesley flaunted his high learning and used it as a show to build an ego, the history of his ministry would read differently than it does. He studied to "Show himself approved," but knew that Christ would smile on Christ-like preaching, the simple gospel.

The greatest evangelist and perhaps the best educated of all times, knew it was powerful works and not pretty words the world needed to produce mighty out-pourings of the Spirit.

"And my speech and my preaching," declared Paul the Apostle, "was not with enticing words of man's wisdom, but in demonstration of the Spirit and power; That your faith should not stand in the wisdom of men, but in the power of God." Paul knew also that enticing words, beautiful words of learned reasoning, could deceive the heart and lead it away from the things of Christ instead of leading it to Christ. To the Colossians he wrote, "Lest any man should beguile you with enticing words."

It can only be speculated what the ministry of Robert Murray McCheyne would have accomplished if he had lived to be an old or even a middle aged man. Having ministered only a little more than seven years, this Scotsman made a lasting impact on the kingdom of God. This young man was so mightily used of God that his father, commenting on the reason for his untimely death, stated he believed God took his son to keep the people from idolizing him.

What was the secret of this man's preaching? What was his approach in presenting the gospel? McCheyene believed in a simple presentation of the message of salvation. "You know," he said, "there is a hell. You know that all the unconverted are hastening to it. You know there is a Savior, and that he is stretching out His hands all day long to sinners. Does it require much learning to tell fellow sinners that they are perishing?"

This statement, perhaps as much as any other, reveals his philosophy of preaching. A simple message delivered in a simple manner brought revival to Dundee, Scotland under the ministry of Robert Murray McCheyne.

In the not so distant past—just one generation ago— an evangelist by the name of Jack Coe was used to fan the flames of revival in many hearts. Those who remember the tent meetings and those who have heard recordings of Jack Coe agree that his message was a simple one. By the thousands, people came, filling to capacity what was billed as "The world's largest gospel tent," to hear such sermons as:
- *Keep knocking*
- *It is Well*
- *Do it Again Lord*

- *Wilt thou be made Whole?*
- *Be of Good Cheer*
- *Detours on the Road to Hell*
- *He will Set Your Fields on Fire.*

Although Coe was a man of learning, having attended a Bible College in Texas, his great crusades were built around these simple sermons. Jack Coe, like McCheyne, died at a young age leaving behind a legacy of revival.

No discussion of simple revival preaching would be complete without reference being made to Uncle Bud Robinson. Uncle Bud, as he was affectionately known, was thought unfit for the ministry by the leaders of the church. Not only was this one—who was destined to become one of God's greatest warriors—illiterate, he was also handicapped by a speech impediment. "Some of the people know what I say, the rest know what I mean" was a remark attributed to him. His goal was not to fill men's heads with creeds and dogmas. He did not seek to illuminate men's lives with a kind of worldly intellectualism. "If we can fill a man's head full of gospel truth." Uncle Bud preached, "It will sink down into his heart and break out on his face and change his whole life." Eternity will reveal the success of this great man of God.

Revival preaching in its simplicity is never vague. There is a certain vividness in preaching that gets results. Those who make such a wide path around the issue, so as never to touch anything, and those who leave a congregation wondering what they are talking about, will never enjoy the fullness of God's blessings. The Spirit surely must lead a man to Christ, but the Spirit should not have to explain to the congregation what the one behind the podium is saying.

Vagueness and elusiveness in the pulpit must cease. Relevant truth must come forth in such a way that nothing is left to be guessed at or figured out.

- Revival comes when preachers paint word pictures with their sermons.
- When the preaching is of the cross, the people must see the cross.
- When heaven is the subject, gates of pearl should be seen.
- Preaching on hell is not effective until those on the pew feel the heat, smell the smoke, and hear the screams.

Revival will never come to a locale so long as sermons are delivered that speak to the sins of people in a distant place. Revival preaching deals with the sins of those present. A study of revivals past bears this out.

Perhaps the most famous sermon ever preached, since Christ preached the Sermon on the Mount, is *Sinners in the Hands of an Angry God.* This sermon was preached by Jonathan Edwards in Northampton, Massachusetts, and the results of it are prime examples of vivid, pointed preaching and what it will produce.

In this famous sermon, Edwards spoke to, "All that were never born again and made new creatures, and raised from being dead in sin to a state of new and before altogether unexperienced light and life." Telling them they were, "In the hands of an angry God. Tis nothing but His mere pleasure that keeps you from being this moment swallowed up in everlasting destruction." He proceeded to say, "The God that holds you over the pit of hell much as one holds a spider or some loathsome insect over the fire, abhors you, and is dreadfully provoked; His wrath toward you burns like fire; you are ten thousand times so abominable in his eyes as the most hateful and venomous serpent is in ours." With no letup Edwards continued to expound on this subject. He spoke of the sinner as if he was a spider suspended over the flames of hell. "You hang by a slender thread, with the flames of divine wrath flashing about it, and ready every moment to singe and burn it asunder; and you have nothing to lay hold of to save yourself, nothing to keep off the flames of wrath, nothing of your own, nothing that you have ever done, nothing that you can do, to induce God to spare you one moment."

This scene became so real in the hearts and minds of the people that they began to grasp the pillars of the building and the pews on which they were sitting, to keep from falling into this awful pit.

No one left that service wondering what the preacher meant or who he was speaking of. All too often this is the case as the minister tries to straddle the proverbial fence. More concern for the comfort of the hearers than for their salvation, has resulted in continued deadness of the church.

The picture was plain. No analysis of the sermon was needed. Even children could see the spider as he hung by a single thread over the flames. In his helpless condition, without someone to save him, the spider would soon perish.

In this and other sermons, this fearless messenger did not tell the congregation how others were about to perish. The messages were pointed.

- **You** are the one being held over the pit of hell.
- **You** are the one God abhors.
- God's wrath burns towards **you**.

Although this sermon, "Sinners in the Hands of an Angry God," was a literary masterpiece, it was in no way complicated or confusing. The truth was proclaimed in a manner that all but the youngest child or the mentally incompetent could grasp it. Jonathan Edwards simply told the congregation that without a born again experience that comes only from Christ, hell was their destination, and there was not a thing they could do about it.

Their works would not keep them from this awful pit. Riches nor prestige could save them. Only the saving grace of Christ could rescue them.

Smart men of religion frown on this type preaching in today's pulpit. Dead church members, cloaked in self-righteousness while living in sin and open rebellion, are hostile toward it. But history proves it to be revival preaching. God smiles on it.

Into the town of Northampton, Massachusetts, revival came. Not a three day meeting, but real revival. One of the first to be converted was a young woman with a shady reputation. The news of her conversion quickly spread over town. The Awakening had begun.

Writing in his *Narrative of Surprising Conversions*, Edwards had this to say, "A great and earnest concern about the great things of religion and the eternal world became universal in all parts of the town, and among persons of all degrees and all ages; the noise among the dry bones waxed louder and louder; all other talk but about spiritual and eternal things was soon thrown by."

- The sounds of prayer could be heard coming from the homes where the people had gathered.
- Closed signs hung from the doors of many business establishments as the proprietors attended to spiritual business.
- Better than one-fourth of the town's population was converted in six months.
- The fire spread.
- It was not long before dozens of communities were enjoying revival blessings.

George Whitefield, a colleague of the Wesley's in England, also enjoyed revival fruit for his labor as he too painted pictures with words. Once he compared a sinner with a poor beggar wandering on the edge of a cliff. As the blind beggar stumbled forward he dropped his cane into the canyon below. Unaware of the danger, he stooped to retrieve it. Caught up in the vividness, someone screamed, "He's gone! He's gone!"

This time of revival known as the Great Awakening, which featured the ministries of Edwards, Whitefield, and others, saw more than hardened sinners saved. Many among the clergy were converted. After hearing Whitefield speak on the subject of unconverted persons in the ministry, an old minister confessed through his tears, "I have been a scholar and have preached the doctrines of grace for a long time. But I believe I have never felt the power of them in my own soul."

Revival preaching does not leave people dangling in confusion. It brings them to a point of decision.
- Yes or no?
- Heaven or hell?
- Christ or Satan?

Revival preaching demands an answer. All do not choose to be saved, but all must make a choice. Revival does not happen in ministries that do not demand a decision.

The year was 1824. The town was Evans Mills, New York. The speaker was Charles Finney. "You who are now willing to pledge to me and to Christ that you will, immediately, make your peace with God, please rise. You that mean that I should understand that you're committed to remain in your present attitude, not to accept Christ, those of you that are of this mind may sit still."

Every individual was forced to make the choice. No one left that meeting wondering where they stood. Accepting or rejecting Christ were the only options.

The townspeople at first were angered by this approach, for it exposed many professing Christians who were not willing to commit themselves. There were now two groups in town:
- those who accepted salvation
- those who rejected it.

Revival **always** brings this separation. Anger reached such a pitch that talk of tarring and feathering Finney circulated through town.

God intervened, honored his servant, sent conviction and revival came to Evans Mills, New York.

It was compassion for the lost that caused these giants of old to be fearless and bold. Some would deny any element of compassion existed in the ministries of men such as Edwards, Whitefield, Finney, Cartwright, Dowie, Wigglesworth, and others. This same group would not be able to see compassion in Christ's motives as he took a small whip and cleansed the temple. But compassion it was that moved him. Compassion for the "blind and the lame" that could not get into the temple because of the money changers and those that bought and sold, put the Savior into action.

Visions of souls lost for eternity—that the religious system is doing nothing to bring to Christ—stir the heart of the revivalist. Compassionate zeal rises up in the bosom of such a one, to the point that nothing else matters.

- Popular acceptance no longer matters.
- Praise of men no longer matters.
- Public opinion no longer matters
- Gold loses its glitter.
- Silver no longer shines.
- The cry becomes, "Give me souls or let me die."
- Five minute prayers turn into hours of prayer.
- Instead of just having daily devotion, these devote their entire lives to Christ.
- Sermons become messages from God to the heart of the hearers.
- Sin and Satan are recognized as the enemy.
- They are attacked with vengeance in every service.

With a spiritual eye, these revivalists see the destroyer.

It is not hatred that causes one to tell others of their sins. It is compassion.

Compassion has come to mean, in modern society, something that it does not mean at all. Humanists would have compassion to mean that a situation—so long as the persons involved are content—should be accepted as it is and no attempt should be made to change it.

This is not true.

For some unexplainable reason, children enjoy playing with fire. It is not compassionate to allow children to play with fire simply because they enjoy it. True compassion sees danger and—with no thought of self—seeks to right the situation.

This was true with a shepherd named David. Seeing the forces of destruction among the flock in the form of a lion and a bear, David, thinking not of his own welfare and safety, but of the flock only, went into action and slew the lion and the bear.

The shepherd that does not respond in this fashion is no shepherd but a hireling. The shepherd, "giveth his life for the sheep."

Revival will come when there is a return to revival preaching. Revival preaching will return when God can find those who will give their all in selfless sacrifice to the ministry.

Chapter 6
Selfless Sacrifice

How few there are that are willing to make any sacrifice to secure the freedom of souls that Jesus so freely offers. - Amanda Smith.

Mrs. Smith knew the true meaning of the word sacrifice. Her soul winning ministry, with its emphasis on holiness of life and sanctification of the heart, spanned four continents.

This was a tremendous feat especially when the obstacles she was forced to overcome are taken into consideration. Being a black, female slave was not the ideal start for one destined to become an international evangelist. Mrs. Smith refused to allow the prejudices of Nineteenth Century America to stop her work for God.

Enduring the shame of slavery, the inequity of racism, and discrimination against her feminine gender, she spent the later years of her life winning souls for Christ. A willingness to sacrifice her entire being to God and His work was rewarded in this world by revival results and in the next world with a crown of life.

Those whose names history records as great revivalists, are those who were willing to "present their bodies a living sacrifice" to God and His will.

Revivalists from the pages of history came from many different cultures and walks of life.

- Finney was a lawyer.
- Moody was a shoe salesman.
- Wigglesworth was a plumber.
- Billy Sunday was a professional athlete.
- John Bunyan was a tinker.
- Jonathan Edwards was a preacher.
- Wesley was educated.
- Uncle Bud Robinson was illiterate.

Different though they were, these all had one thing in common: they were willing to sacrifice themselves and all they had for the sake of revival.

Revival never comes to the selfish, only to the selfless. Only those who are willing to forsake all and follow Christ will enjoy the fruits of revival. Only those who "let the dead bury the dead," can follow our Lord in the fullness of His power.

Elishas can be found only among those who are willing to kill the oxen and burn the plow. Insisting on keeping the oxen in the stall and the plow in the barn, will prevent one from picking up the mantle. Only those who refuse to be turned back have the right to ask for a "double portion". "Where Is the Lord God of Elijah?" can come only from the lips of those who make a total commitment.

Seeking first the Kingdom of God and His righteous will add the blessings of God. Seeking comfort and ease for self first, will subtract the blessings of the Lord.

Isaac knew, that day on the way to the land of Moriah, that having wood and fire was not enough. Something was missing. "Where is the sacrifice?" was the question he asked Abraham.

It is the pertinent question for the church today. If wood represents material things, there is no lack. If fire, in this application, means ability, there is not shortage. But where is the sacrifice? Or, more accurately and to the point, where are those willing to sacrifice to see real revival? The wood and the fire are not enough.

Sacrifice is an absolute necessity to revival.

Past generations have known and applied this truth. In doing so, many suffered but the suffering could not compare with the glory that was manifested to them. The pains of sacrifice vanished as souls were swept into the kingdom.

This generation will never witness the things Finney, Moody, Wigglesworth and others witnessed until it is willing to deny itself as they did.

Early in his ministry, D. L. Moody acquired the nickname, "Crazy Moody." There is some debate as to how this came about.

Arthur Percy Fitt, Mr. Moody's son-in-law, gives this reason in his book *The Shorter Life of D. L. Moody*. "People began to call him "Crazy Moody" because he left a lucrative position in the shoe business to serve the lord without a salary. He gave up business for personal profit once for all and never after tried to accumulate wealth."

D. L. Moody went to Chicago with one thing in mind. His ambition was to become a wealthy man. Hard work and determination paid off, and soon he began amassing his fortune.

After becoming a Christian, Moody began to serve the Lord as a Sunday school teacher. All went well until the day another Sunday school teacher, who was sick and knew his time was short, asked Moody to help win his students to Christ. From house to house and place to place, went the ailing teacher and the shoe salesman, telling of the saving grace of Jesus. They did not stop until the last student was converted.

Never the same was D. L. Moody after this soul-winning experience. His ambition changed from money to souls.

"I didn't know what this was going to cost me," Moody said. "I was disqualified for business. It had become distasteful to me. I had gotten a taste of another world, and cared no more for making money. For some days after, the greatest struggle of my life took place. Should I give up business and give myself wholly to Christian work, or should I not? God helped me to decide aright, and I have never regretted my choice."

The rest of the D. L. Moody story, with all its victories, is forever preserved in the pages of history.

Moody's story, though different in circumstance, was not unlike one that preceded his by a few years. In Adams, New York, a twenty-nine year old lawyer, Charles Grandison Finney, had passed through the same vale. After a marvelous conversion, the call to preach the gospel rang clear in his heart. "This at first stumbled me," confessed Finney, "but now after receiving the baptism of the Spirit, I was quite willing to preach the gospel. Nay, I found that I was unwilling to do anything else. I had no longer any desire to practice law. I had no disposition to make money. I had no hungering and thirsting after worldly pleasures and amusements in any direction. Nothing, it seemed, could be put in competition with the worth of a soul; and no labor could be so sweet as that of holding up Christ to a dying world."

Many have said that the lawyer who left the court room where civil cases were tried, and entered the court room where the cases were spiritual was perhaps the greatest revivalist of all times. Many are the souls who will rise in eternity to call this man blessed. Education, the cost of education, social status, wealth and all the other things that go along with the lawyer's profession were sacrificed for the sake of the Gospel.

This sacrifice did not go unnoticed. Heaven smiled on it. God blessed it. And thousands of souls were the benefactors of it.

In 1907 the president of a large insurance company said to one of the top executives of the company, "You have worked hard, Lake. You need a change. Take a vacation for three months, and if you want to preach, preach. But at the end of three months, fifty-thousand-dollars a year will look like a lot of money to you, and you will have little desire to sacrifice it for the dreams of religious possibilities." These words were spoken to Rev. John G. Lake.

To read the story of John G. Lake, is to read something akin to the Book of Acts. As a missionary to South Africa and also an evangelist and pastor in the United States, Lake's ministry was marked by the miraculous. To simply say that revival came where this man of God ministered would be an understatement. Much material has been published, detailing this man and his work for God. It is time well spent for those who would read the accounts of God's blessing on this man.

The present purpose is not to detail the results of Lake's ministry, but to show how he came to have such a phenomenal ministry.

Having had an experience with God that was glorious, to say the least, Lake knew that God had called him. For a period of time he continued to hold his secular position, which was very profitable, while also preaching the gospel. "The desire to proclaim the message of Christ," Lake said, "and demonstrate His power to save and bless, grew in my soul until my life was swayed by this overwhelming passion."

After continuing for some time with—as Mr. Lake stated—"my heart divided," he decided to talk with the company president about the matter. It was at this time that the proposition, before mentioned, was presented to him for consideration. Lake's own relating of the events of that three months is thrilling to the hearts of those who cherish real revival. "I thanked him, accepted an invitation to join a brother in evangelistic work, and left the office, never to return.

"During the three months, I preached every day to large congregations, saw a multitude of people saved from their sins and healed of their diseases, and hundreds of them baptized in the Holy Ghost. At the end of three months, I said to God, I am through forever with everything in life but the proclamation and demonstration of the Gospel of Jesus Christ.

"I disposed of my estate and distributed my funds in a

manner I believed to be in the best interests of the Kingdom of God, made myself wholly dependent upon God for the support of myself and my family, and abandoned myself to the preaching of Jesus."

The company president, thinking there would be little desire to sacrifice a large salary for "the dreams of religious possibilities," had underestimated the resolve of one who loved his Savior and desired to do His will. For a few years, the earthly realm witnessed the wonderful works of God wrought at the hands of John G. Lake. Many are the exciting testimonies of those touched through the ministry of this man, who thought providing assurance for the spiritual was better than selling insurance for the natural.

"I saw Charley swing hard," Billy Sunday remembered, "and heard the bat hit the ball with a terrific boom. Bennett had smashed the ball on the nose. I saw the ball rise in the air and knew it was going clear over my head. I could judge within ten feet of where the ball would light. I turned my back to the ball and ran.

"The field was crowded with people; I yelled, 'Stand back!' And that crowd opened as the Red Sea opened for the rod of Moses. I ran on, and as I ran I made a prayer; it wasn't theological, either. I said, 'God, if you ever helped mortal man, help me to get that ball, and you haven't very much time to make up your mind either.' I ran and jumped over the bench and stopped."

"I thought I was close enough to catch it. I looked back and saw it was going over my head. I jumped and shoved out my left hand and the ball hit and stuck. At the rate I was going the momentum carried me on and I fell under the feet of a team of horses. I jumped up with the ball in my hand."

Billy Sunday—a professional baseball player—had become a Christian. Already he was learning the benefits of prayer.

It wasn't long, however, before the object of his prayers was not a baseball that he wanted to catch but rather souls of humanity that he wanted to lead to Christ. For four years he sought to combine his career and his Christian service. His deep convictions led to his refusing to play ball on Sundays. Instead, as his team was on the ball field on the Lord's Day, Billy Sunday would be on the gospel field, speaking, preaching and working for the Lord.

It became increasingly apparent to Billy Sunday that if he was to please God, he would have to leave the sport he loved. In March 1891, the decision was made. This young athlete rejected what has been called "a fat contract" and became a member of God's Gospel Team.

Denying himself the career, the money, the cheers of the crowd, Billy Sunday sold out to God.

"I went to work for the Y.M.C.A. and had a very hard time of it. It was during those hard times that I hardly had enough to pay my house rent, but I stuck to my promise," Billy Sunday said.

God also stuck to his promise and before long blessings more abundant were being poured out in revivals where a ballplayer turned preacher was doing the preaching. Billy Sunday was no longer trying to hit a "home run." He was helping souls make the "run home." It has been estimated that as many as one-million souls were won for the Kingdom through the ministry of Billy Sunday. Baseball could never have presented him with a crown compared with the one he received as death carried him into the presence of his God. The God that he sacrificed all to follow.

Perhaps now, more than ever before, there is need for revival. The fire of Heaven burning on the altar is the only hope of a generation turned from truth. Religious ceremony has not and will not convince men to turn from their evil ways. Only when God answers by fire are men convinced that he is Lord. Elijah knew on Mount Carmel nothing less than fire falling from heaven would convince Israel that Jehovah was God. The prophet rebuilt the altar, placed the sacrifice on it, and the fire fell.

Revival fire does not fall on empty altars. Only those altars where a sacrifice has been placed will experience revival.

God is still God. He has not changed. The God of Moody, Finney, Lake and Sunday is still alive and well. His Throne is still high above every evil force. He is all powerful. His grace is sufficient.

Where is the God of Moody, Finney, Lake and Sunday? This is not the question. The question is, where are the Moodys, Finneys, Lakes and Sundays who will make a selfless sacrifice for the Kingdom?

In a small Missouri town near the mid-point of the twentieth century, the truth that God was looking for a man who would make a total commitment dawned on a young preacher. Gayle Jackson was struck by the Words of Jesus, "Howbeit, this kind goeth not out but by prayer and fasting."

One afternoon this young man spoke to his wife, "God is calling me to go out and set the captives free, but I must first prepare myself. My preparations may take me near to death, and I do not know where and when it will end, but you need not prepare any food for me until I let you know."

A sacrifice was laid on the altar. The Fire of God began to fall. In the summer of 1950 in a crusade in New Orleans, Louisiana, it was reported five-thousand-six-hundred-eighty-two souls were born again. Results similar to these were reported from revivals in Mobile Alabama, Dothan Alabama, Meridian Mississippi, Biloxi Mississippi, Dallas Texas and many other places.

Empty altars are the curse of the church. Bare altars are cold altars. Clean, sanitary altars unsoiled by sacrifice, will never know fire. God does not honor the altar. Glory does not fall on the altar. The fire of revival falls on the sacrifice that has been placed on the altar.

The name John Knox is familiar to students of church and religious history. His reputation as "The Thundering Scot," is widely known but few know of George Wishart, the man whose life inspired Knox. John Knox had his beginning in gospel work as a bodyguard to George Wishart. This time of service and the eventual slaying of Wishart by the authorities, tempered Knox. This hardening of his resolve served John Knox well in the years of his ministry.

It was George Wishart's willingness to lay self on the altar that made the young Scotsman who guarded him willing to take up the torch at his death. Not only did Wishart make the supreme sacrifice in his death, during his life he gave up one meal in three and one day in four to fasting. The religious climate of Scotland was changed forever.

The need is revival. The land must be healed. The secret is selfless sacrifice.

In 1872 Henry Varley of Australia made a statement at a prayer meeting in London. D. L. Moody heard that statement and the impact was lasting. The present generation needs to hear again those words.

"The world has yet to see," Varley said, "what God will do with a man wholly consecrated to Him."

While the church "waits on the Lord," the Lord is searching for "a man among them that should make up the hedge and stand in the gap."

Those who are willing to sacrifice for revival, must also be willing to "endure hardness as a good soldier." Persecution will come, but so will revival.

Chapter 7
Enduring Hardness

Come, be of good cheer. Let us not be daunted. Our cause is good. We need not be ashamed of it; to preach God's word is so good a work that we shall be well rewarded even if we suffer for it. ~ **John Bunyan**

Studying the giants of past revivals reveals many truths. One of these being that suffering and persecution come to those who are used of God.

Jesus said, "Blessed are ye when men shall revile you and persecute you and shall say all manner of evil against you falsely for my sake."

Revival always brings opposition. It is not possible to have it otherwise. Only those who are willing to deny themselves and take up their cross of suffering, need look for an outpouring of the Spirit.

The opening words of this chapter illustrate the proper attitude for those who seek spiritual awakening. John Bunyan spoke these words in response to those who tried to persuade him not to hold service after it was learned he would be arrested for doing so.

Counting the preaching of God's Word, "so good a work," this man of God preached in spite of the threat. The authorities were good to their word. In the course of the service, Mr. Bunyan was arrested.

Describing his appearance before the judge, this great pilgrim said, "Before I went down to the Justice, I begged of God that His will be done. For I was not without hopes my imprisonment might be an awakening to the saints in this country. And verily at my return, I did sweetly meet my God in the prison."

One would have to possess a holy passion for the things of God to make such a statement. John Bunyan of Bedford, England was such a man. The name John Bunyan will be known as long as the church inhabits this world and when the church moves to the other world, it will be immortal. It was this man who gave the world the great literary work, *The Pilgrim's Progress*.

Translated into more than one-hundred languages, *The Pilgrim's Progress* is second in popularity only to the Bible. This great book was not Bunyan's only contribution to Christianity but it is the one most remembered. Not the least of his gifts to the Christian Church was his example of steadfastness in persecution.

Born in 1628, Bunyan followed his father's profession as a tinker. A tinker, one who mends pots and pans, usually traveled from place to place in the pursuit of employment. Being a tinker placed one at the lower end of the social scale.

God, who does not regard social standings, began dealing with this man from Bedford. After a long struggle, Bunyan found peace with his creator. After conversion, he began to preach. Crowds would gather to hear the uneducated tinker preach.

"This man is not chosen out of an earthly but out of the heavenly university, the church of Christ. He hath taken these three heavenly degrees, to wit, union with Christ, the anointing of the Spirit, and experiences of the temptations of Satan, which do more fit a man for that mighty work of preaching the Gospel than all university learning and degrees that can be had," said a member of the learned clergy of John Bunyan.

However, all the rulers of the land and of the church, were not so sympathetic. Their hostile spirit resulted in Bunyan's arrest in 1660. The charge, though elaborate in its wording, was basically for preaching without a license.

Standing steadfast, this man of conviction refused freedom when it was offered in exchange for a pledge not to preach. Speaking of his conversation with the judge concerning this matter, Bunyan said, "I told him as to this matter, I was at a point with him; for if I was out of prison today, I would preach the Gospel again tomorrow, by the help of God."

This uncompromising stand turned what would have been a three months sentence into approximately twelve years in prison.

The suffering was intense. The agony came not only from the loss of freedom and inability to involve himself in Gospel work as he desired, but there was also his family. The pain is felt in a heart-rending statement made from his prison cell concerning his family. Bunyan said, "I found myself a man encompassed with infirmities. The parting with my wife and poor children hath often been to me, in this place, as the pulling of the flesh from my bones." There were four children and he mourned, "Especially my poor blind child who lay nearer my heart than all I had besides."

Bunyan felt that his actions were "Pulling his house upon the head of his wife and children," but the love of God and the things of God caused him to say, "Yet, thought I, I must do it, I must do it."

Persecution is Satan's attempt to abort revival before it can come to birth and to stop it if it does come. How many books, such as *The Pilgrims Progress*, were never written because the intended author could not endure persecution? How many sermons, such as *Sinners in the Hands of an Angry God* were never preached because of fear in a preacher's heart? In this life there will never be an answer to these questions.

John Bunyan's willingness to suffer and "endure hardness as a good soldier" made him one of religious history's greatest men. He was trustworthy in persecution. Therefore, God could trust him with spiritual gifts. Those who run from the enemy, will never enjoy the fruits of victory.

- God stands with those who stand.
- He never flees with those who flee.
- Faith stands.
- Fear runs.
- It takes faith to please God.

Faith such as the tinker from Bedford had.

Many are the men who desire revival in their churches and meetings such as Charles Finney had. Yet so few are willing to suffer even in the smallest way.

Concentrating on the huge successes of Charles G. Finney, the persecution he confronted is often overlooked. In a letter dated May 11, 1826 Father Nash spoke of Finney and himself being burned in effigy. Relating how the meetings were frequently being disturbed as the opposers would make noise in the house of God, how lies were being reported and written, Father Nash, never-the-less, expressed his faith that the work would go on. Go on it did, because these men of God could not be stopped in their search for revival.

All that can be stopped will be stopped.

Satan tried in vain to abort the revival ministry of Evangelist Jack Coe. Destined to become a leader in the great salvation-healing revival that swept America in the middle of the twentieth century, Jack Coe was severely tried.

This man of God suffered both mentally and physically. While serving in the armed forces of the United States, Jack Coe spent time in the "crazy ward", as he labeled it, at least seven times. One of those times he stayed nine days.

His religious convictions were the reason behind these actions. Because he would pray and preach in the barracks and could be heard praising God while standing in line, he was thought to be insane.

Knowing that upon his discharge from the armed forces, Jack Coe would be used to bring revival to the land, the enemy set out to destroy his faith. It didn't work that way. His faith was strengthened, not weakened. By refusing to give in to the pressures around him, he learned an important lesson. God will take care of His own.

Learning this lesson served Jack Coe well during the years in his ministry. Leaving the armed forces, Coe launched out into one of the greatest salvation-healing revivals known since the days of the apostles. Beginning small, this ministry quickly grew. Jack Coe himself described it as going from "Pup Tent to World's largest Gospel Tent." Opposition grew also. Enemies of the gospel fought with increasing intensity the message of the atonement of Christ. Divine healing is a part of the atonement. This, the scripture teaches.

Cold, dead ministries would not stand by and watch revival sweep through the ranks of the faithful. Thousands were saved and healed as they trusted the finished work of the cross. Miracles abounded to the dismay of the lifeless church.

Propaganda campaigns were begun for the purpose of discrediting the ministries of many, especially the ministry of Jack Coe. The more Satan fought, the more the ministries grew. Unable to hinder through subtle means, these distractors turned to the legal system of the American Government.

While conducting a great crusade in Miami, Florida, in 1956, Jack Coe was arrested, jailed and tried. He was charged with practicing medicine without a license. Such a ridiculous charge could not stand in the court system. Revered Coe was found not guilty and released. The man of God endured this suffering and continued his ministry until the time of his untimely death.

This was not the first time this strategy was undertaken by those opposed to revival. John Alexander Dowie was arrested one hundred times for practicing medicine without a license in Chicago.

Persecution follows revival. It is a price that must be paid. Those who love the life of ease should never seek revival. Only those willing to be abused should apply for the job.

John Knox was sentenced to nineteen months in the galleys. Galleys were sailing ships that were also equipped with oars. When the wind did not blow, the ships were rowed. The oars were manned by criminals and prisoners paying their debts to society.

Alongside the thief and murderer labored one whose only crime was preaching the Gospel. Faithful in unjust suffering, Knox was counted worthy. After his release, this revivalist continued to carry the gospel throughout his life. With a devotion that could not be stopped in old age and bad health, he insisted on preaching even though he was not able to mount the pulpit without assistance. His voice became so weak, only those nearest him could hear him, yet he continued faithful to his calling.

Jonathan Edwards was driven from his pulpit and served as a missionary to an Indian tribe.

T. Dewitt Talmadge was brought to public trial by the Presbytery of his denomination, charged with falsehood and deceit. He was found not guilty as it was only a ploy to humiliate and discredit him.

Soft preachers are keeping revival from the church. Feelings that are easily wounded and egos that have to be stroked and petted have robbed a generation of the power of God manifested in revival.

- Where there is an Able, there is a Cain to seek his life.
- Where there is an Elijah, there is a Jezebel to hate him.
- Where there is an Elisha, there are children to mock him.

- Where there is a Nehemiah, there are Sanballats and Tobiahs to oppose him.
- Where there is a Shadrach, there is a Nebuchadnezzar to cast him into the fire.
- Where there is a Daniel, there are presidents and princes to oppose him. There is a lion's den.
- Where there is a John the Baptist, there is a Herodias ready to have his head.
- Where there is a Paul there is a prison cell in which to be bound.

However, where these are, there is real revival. The kind that will heal our land. Oh! For some who would endure hardness as a good soldier!

Chapter 8
Fearless Faith

***Only believe, only believe, all things are possible, only believe.* ~ Paul Rader**

The message of this chorus is the underlying principle of revival. The ability to believe that God will honor His Word with action is an absolute necessity where spiritual renewal is expected.

The giants of revivals past, without exception, were men and women of great faith.
- Some did not have great personalities.
- Some were not great organizers and promoters.
- Some had little or no talent.
- Others did not possess great preaching and speaking abilities,
- But! All had great faith.

A faith that is unafraid is the mark of a revivalist.

No one should ever anticipate anything more than a mediocre experience when strong faith is not present. In the place of seeking revival, many should seek to increase faith. It is the lack of faith that is hindering and blocking a real move of God.

Smith Wigglesworth, The Apostle of Faith, used the chorus "Only Believe" as the theme song of his revival meetings. Above the singing of the congregation, this man of God could be heard thundering out the words, "all things are possible, only believe."

Although his singing left something to be desired, his faith in God was the factor that attracted large crowds to his ministry. Churches and other meeting halls were filled to capacity time and time again. The masses came to see the man who was once a plumber, demonstrate a faith that was unafraid to take on the forces of evil in spiritual combat.

If the chorus, "Only Believe," was Wigglesworth's theme song, then the overall theme of his ministry is revealed in the following statement.

"I am not moved," declared Smith Wigglesworth, "By what I see or hear; I am moved by what I believe."

This was more than a statement of fundamental belief. For this great revivalist, it was a guideline for ministry. Wigglesworth did not minister according to circumstance or appearance. He ministered according to faith.

A cancer patient, accompanied by his physician, was brought to a Wigglesworth meeting to be ministered to. The awful disease had progressed to a point that life was almost gone. On learning that the cancer was in the stomach area, the man of God proceeded to deal with it. A weaker faith would have dealt with the situation differently. Seeing the situation, the frailty of the body and the nearness of death, would have affected the actions of many. The Apostle of Faith was not affected in the least by these things. Making a fist,

Wigglesworth struck the dying man in the stomach. Receiving the blow, the man appeared to die. The doctor reported to Smith Wigglesworth that he had killed the man and assured him he would be sued. Wigglesworth responded, saying, "He is healed." With never a look back he continued down the line ministering to others. Approximately ten minutes later someone tapped Brother Wigglesworth on the back shouting, "I am healed! I am healed!" Recognizing the man—who a few minutes earlier appeared to have died—God's servant instructed him to praise God. His healing was complete. God had honored a faith that was fearless.

While to many it may seem cruel to strike a dying man in the stomach, to Smith Wigglesworth it was the thing to do. His faith told him that man would be healed. He was unafraid.

"Great faith is the product of great fights," Brother Wigglesworth once said. Great faith was what he had.

The newspaper advertisement said, "Bring the dead, I believe what Jesus said." A Wigglesworth meeting was being announced.

Some who read the advertisement decided to take it literally and showed up at the meeting with a corpse. The man of great faith stood the corpse against the wall and commanded it to walk in Jesus name. The corpse promptly fell to the floor. The scene was repeated until life came into the body and the man walked across the platform.

It is impossible for the faint of heart to imagine faith such as this. Only when it is accepted that Jesus is the same now as

He was in the past, can one act with such faith.

Satan knows that to stop faith is to stop revival. For this reason he endeavors to focus the minds of men on circumstances, causing them to be governed by what they see and hear rather than by what God says.

Charles Finney's faith in God was the factor that separated his ministry from the ministries of his contemporaries.

The extraordinary prayer life of this great man of God has already been considered. The reason his prayers "availed much," was faith.

- Finney prayed and believed.
- He prayed and expected something to happen.
- Prayer alone produces nothing.
- The formality of praying does nothing but fill up a space of time in the service.
- Praying and believing equals seeing.

It was with unshakable faith that Finney prayed for rain in the summer of 1853. The area was on the brink of disaster. So severe was the drought, cattle would soon die. Crop failure was imminent. Financial ruin, as well as hunger, loomed before the populace like some giant monster. Day by day it crept closer until it seemed there was no hope. Pain and suffering would be intense. Death would be slow and agonizing.

Few smiles could be detected as the worshippers filled the pews that summer, Sunday morning. Another day had dawned—without a cloud in sight. The sun beamed down with merciless heat sapping up any remaining moisture. Not one person anticipated rain. Not one drop was expected.

Arising from his chair, the minister walked to the pulpit. Sensing the mood of the people, Charles Finney lifted his voice into prayer to God.

"O Lord! Send us rain," he cried. "We pray for rain. Our harvests perish. There is not a drop for the thirsting birds. The ground is parched. The choking cattle lift their voices toward a brassy heaven and lowing, cry, 'Lord give us water'. We do not presume to dictate to Thee what is best for us, yet Thou doest invite us to come to Thee as children to a father and tell Thee all our wants. We want rain! Even the squirrels in the woods are suffering for want of it. Unless Thou givest us rain our cattle must die. O Lord, send us rain! And send it now! For Jesus sake! Amen!"

This prayer contained the faith and expectancy of an Elijah.

The pastor then took his text, "I have somewhat against thee because thou hast left thy first love." He had been preaching for only a few minutes on the subject, "Hewing close to the line," when a cloud about the size of a man's hand appeared in the sky. The small cloud grew fast. The shutters of the church began to rattle in the wind. Despair vanished and joyful anticipation took its place. Great drops of rain began to fall from the sky that only a few minutes before knew nothing but the sun.

The sermon was never finished. "Let us thank the Lord for the rain," admonished the man of God. The sound of weeping rose from the congregation as praise poured forth to the almighty. The service was dismissed and a happy group of people splashed their way home. This was not the end of the story, however.

That afternoon the building was once again packed to hear Charles Finney preach. "I have never witnessed so solemn a scene," commented one who was there. At the close of the message the response came from all over the building. From the galleries they came. Choir members left their places in the choir loft and came. It was estimated that one thousand came to the altar of repentance that Sunday afternoon. One of these being the great colored orator, Frederick Douglass.

Frederick Douglass spoke, "When I was young and a slave, Mr. Finney, when my back quivered under the master's lash, I clung close to God and felt the comfort of true religion. But prosperity has been too much for me, and I have come under the dominion of the world, and have lost my first love."

Finney wept aloud crying, "God bless you, Brother Douglass! God bless you!"

This great harvest of souls was not the result of Charles Finney's preaching abilities alone. A child-like faith that could unlock the gates of heaven had produced rain, physical rain and spiritual rain.

Finney was a master in his ability to produce revival, because he had mastered the ability to believe God. Believing God would stand by His Word and do what He promised, was the key to success for this man who is hailed by many as the greatest revivalist of all times.

The capability to pray and receive an answer was not the only way faith benefited past masters of revival. This faith allowed them to envision the field of harvest. This vision of the harvest moved them in the direction God would have them go. While others sat and waited, the great ones moved.

The ability to move by faith separates
- the uncommon from the common
- the mighty from the weak
- the great from the small.

Walking by sight never produced anything for the glory of God. This is the natural way. God deals in the supernatural. The Almighty leads His people to the water where there is no bridge. He then causes the water to part and makes a way across. Leading His children to a wilderness where there is no bread, He feeds them from heaven, angel food—manna.

Following the Master into the desert can only mean one thing, water will come pouring from a Rock.

The miracles, the manna, and the water, are missing from many churches and ministries today. Being led by sight instead of by faith is the cause.

- Looking for the bridge stops the miracle of deliverance.
- Staying near the supermarket, holds back the manna.
- Refusing to leave the source of natural water takes away the opportunity to drink supernatural water.

Abram had this faith. The scripture said, "When he was called…he went out, not knowing whether he went."

This action brought tremendous blessing to this Patriarch. His name was changed from Abram, "Exalted Father," to Abraham, "Father of a Multitude." A man with one heir can be esteemed by that single individual and become an exalted father. To be the father of a multitude, is quite another thing.

- Faith moved the Apostle Paul to Macedonia after their cry for help was heard in a vision.
- Visions of the harvest led Moody from a shoe store.

- Finney from the court room.
- Wigglesworth from his plumber's trade.
- and John G. Lake from his executive position.

Traveling to South Africa with no prior arrangements for lodging and provisions, would be considered illogical to the natural mind. John G. Lake did this exact thing. Hearing the call of God, he took his wife and seven children to that far away continent, having nothing but faith. The only knowledge he possessed was that God would provide. "Upon our arrival at Johannesburg, Lake relates the story, I observed a little woman bustling up. She said, "You are an American missionary party?"

The reply was, "Yes."

Addressing me, she said, "How many are there in your family?"

I answered, "My wife, myself and seven children."

"Oh," she said. "You are the family. The Lord has sent me to meet you, and I want to give you a home."

"That same afternoon," Lake said, "we were living in a furnished cottage in the suburbs."

Gordon Lindsay, in his book, *John G. Lake, Apostle to Africa*, tells how this servant of Christ went to Africa without funds. "Every mile of the journey was a miracle. Within five years the message they (Lake and his co-worker Hezrnelhalch) brought, had penetrated to the remote areas of South Africa. An apostolic revival broke out of such power that in a short time hundreds of churches and missions were established throughout the land."

This great man, and others, possessed a fearless faith.
- Faith their prayers would be answered.
- Faith to see the harvest.
- Faith to move in any direction God pointed.
- Faith to trust their Lord to supply all their needs.
- Faith to not give up when things seemed to go wrong.

This faith is an absolute requirement to see revival. Without it nothing happens. Things remain the same. Nothing changes in the absence of faith. God is not moved by methods, programs or talent. Faith in the heart of the believer is the thing that moves God.

The mechanics of revival are well known to this generation. Well trained and well equipped describes ministries of this day. What is lacking? What is the missing ingredient? What is holding back the great surge of revival? The lack of faith! Fearless faith!

Chapter 9
Revival Killers

Revival is a time of great spiritual crisis and is thus fraught with great spiritual dangers. The devil will seek to imitate the work of the Spirit. The believer must walk carefully and humbly before God. He must know how to cooperate with the Third Person of the Trinity during this spiritual floodtide. ~ **James A. Stewart (Revival Challenge found in the book** *Rent Heavens* ~ **an account of the Welsh revival of 1904)**

The Welsh revival lasted for a period of approximately two years. The other great revival of the early twentieth century—the Azusa Street Revival—lasted approximately three and one-half years.

Studying these great out-pourings of the Spirit is something akin to reading the New Testament. Signs, wonders, and miracles abounded. The effects of both these awakenings spread around the world. This happened without the help of radio, television, or tape recording equipment. The only media available to these pioneer revivalists was the printed page.

The fire of revival crossed oceans and continents for the

glory of God. There can be no doubt that these revivals were the work of God. Man could never have wrought such marvelous things. God, and only God, could produce anything of the magnitude of these great moves of the Spirit, yet they were short lived.

What would have been the results if these revivals had lasted?

- The world, and especially the church world, would not be in the condition it is in today.
- Truth would not be fallen in the street, and heathenism would not be the order of the day.
- Babies would not be aborted by the tens of thousands.
- Same sex marriages would not be taking place.
- Homes and families would be staying together.
- Murder, rape, and incest would be forgotten crimes.
- Churches would be filled to capacity every service.
- Men would love their neighbor as themselves and would treat others as they would like to be treated.

The truth is they did not last. The fire died. The altars grew cold. The lamp went out in the Temple. Revival killers were present and did their awful work.

During times of revival, James A. Steward said, "All hell is awake and working." This is a true statement. Hell relaxes when the church sleeps.

When the church arouses, Hell awakens itself and goes to work. Revival alarms the Devil. Nothing is so despised in

Hell as a spiritual awakening. Everything possible is done to prevent it and once it comes, everything possible is done to stop it.

Since unity of the body of Christ is one of the chief requirements of revival, one of the greatest revival killers is division in the body of Christ.

Division and strife were the root causes of the demise of the Welsh and Azusa revivals.

When revival comes, all involved must guard against this evil spirit. Maintaining a constant prayer life, esteeming every man's brother better than himself, and walking in the spirit of humility will safeguard against this revival killer. Doing one's part with all thy might and letting God take care of other's shortcomings, is a great cure for division in the body. Each individual finding their proper position—whether it be a position of leadership or some other—and filling it, brings victory over this terrible destroyer.

It has been said, "On the day of battle one and the same feeling animates every bosom; after the victory they become divided."

It is easier for some to pray together than to worship together. Many who unite themselves in prayer, separate over the answer to that prayer. Problems unite. Prosperity, too often, separates.

As it became evident that the Azusa Street revival was beginning to cool off, Frank Bartleman made this statement. "The battle from the beginning, both in Los Angeles and elsewhere, has been the conflict between the flesh and the spirit, between Ishmael and Isaac."

The flesh, in the time of revival, is tempted to become proud and egotistical. As God uses an individual, Satan tempts that one to think it is something of their doing or ability.

Humility before God brings revival. Pride kills it.

In November, 1904, R. A. Torrey wrote to Evan Roberts. "I cannot tell you the joy that has come to my heart, as I have read of the mighty work of God in Wales. I am praying that God will keep you, simply trusting in Him, and obedient to Him, going not where men shall call you but going where He shall lead you, and that He may keep you humble. It is so easy for us to become exalted when God uses us as the instruments of His power. It is so easy to think that we are something ourselves, and when we get to thinking that, God will set us aside. May God keep you humble, and fill you more and more with His mighty power."

John Bunyan, replying to some who wanted to know what he preferred to be called said, "Since you desire to know by what name I wish to be called, I desire, if God should count me worthy, to be called a Christian, a believer, or any other name sanctioned by the Holy Ghost."

This attitude will keep the revival killers, pride and egoism at bay.

John Alexander Dowie had this righteous attitude during his early years in Chicago. When some told him his ministry resembled that of an apostle's, he replied with honesty and humility. "I do not think that I have reached a deep enough depth of true humility. I do not think I have reached a deep enough depth of true abasement and self-effacement, for the high office of an apostle. In the question of becoming an apostle, it is not the question of rising high, it is the question of becoming low enough."

When Dowie was approached by some who claimed that God had revealed to them that he was Elijah the Restorer, whose coming to earth was prophesied in the New Testament, he soundly rebuked them, removed them from his presence and warned them never to mention this thing again.

With such a spirit of humility, it is no wonder that God blessed and used this man. Greater and greater victories were won. Thousands were saved, healed and delivered at the hands of this humble servant. Then the revival killer shot his arrow of pride. The intended target was John Alexander Dowie's heart.

The poisoned dart found its mark.

In June 1901, this man who had risen from obscurity to a place of prominence, declared that he was Elijah the Restorer. He related how a strange and intense conviction had come into his consciousness that he was indeed Elijah, the one spoken of by the prophets. It was now only a matter of time before this man, mightily used of God, would die in disgrace. A simple stone marks his grave in a small cemetery in the city he founded in Zion, Illinois.

Boasting, self-edification, and self-righteousness are killers that have destroyed many moves of the spirit. The story is told of one evangelist, after a meeting in Jamaica, reporting about twice as many converts as the total population of the country. Over blown statistics have caused more than one revival wind to cease.

Differing opinions and ideas do not kill revival in themselves. It is when individuals feel that their opinions and ideas are the only right ones and everyone else should share them that they become killers.

John Wesley wrote, "I am sick of opinions. Give me a humble, gentle, lover of God and man, a man full of mercy and good fruits; without partiality or hypocrisy. Let my soul be with such Christians, wheresoever they are and whatsoever opinion they are of. Whosoever doeth the will of my father, the same is my brother."

Stubbornness and demanding one's rights, will destroy any move of the Spirit. When there are those present who would see revival die rather than submit themselves to the wishes or authority of others, the Dove will fly away. There must be a love for the revival that goes deeper than love of our own feelings.

The story of King Solomon, two mothers and one living child, illustrates this point. To settle the argument of who the child belonged to, who had the right to claim it, Solomon decreed that the child would be divided. Of course, to divide it would kill it. One preferred killing the child rather than seeing the other have it. The other preferred to see the child live, even if it meant denying herself of what was rightfully hers. Loving the child more than loving self, preserved the child alive. Anything else, and there would have been a funeral.

Two churches sit on opposite sides of the road not far from one another in a rural southern community. A stone could almost be thrown from one to the other. Once neither of them existed. Then a minister with a burden came. A brush arbor was constructed. The fires of revival came to this out-of-the-way place. A church was established as God continued to bless. After some time two different hymn books were acquired by the congregation. Some began to prefer one book over the other and would not participate in worship unless their favorite was used. Now there are two churches. The revival was sacrificed. All these things are revival killers. The glory of God cannot exist where these are found:

- Learning how to perform religious acts, such as preaching and singing instead of being dependent on the anointing.
- Forgetting how to pray.
- Replacing the prayer room with the party room.
- Taking glory that belongs to God and giving it to man.
- A jealous spirit.
- Laziness.
- Taking the blessing of the Lord for granted.

It is time to kill the killer and destroy the destroyer, letting the glory of God ring out one more time!

Chapter 10
In Conclusion

Lord send revival or we perish. **~ This should be the prayer of every Christian.**

The destroyer has come. Homes, churches, schools and society itself is being dragged into Hell. As the religious community grows colder, Hell grows hotter. Iniquity is abounding because the love of many has waxed cold.

Considering conditions existing in too many churches today will prove the point that revival is sorely needed.

- Pastors who are more concerned about their golf scores than they are of the souls of humanity; this is a curse on our land.
- Church leaders showing more concern for the treasury than they do for things eternal are selling a generation to the Devil.
- Parents who would rather see their daughters on the cheerleading squad or their sons on the ball team than in the altar are squandering the children of this generation.
- Christians sitting on pews today who have never seen real revival; they have heard, but they

have never been witnesses to the power of God.
- Preacher's children growing up in the church but having no desire for God or spiritual things. Daddy preaches it but does not live it.
- Carnal minds running the church.
- Churches being run like a business.
- Crowds wanted for their money and to make the preacher and church look successful.
- Conversions becoming so rare, the altars have been removed from the sanctuary.
- Communion losing its sacredness, it is now a mere formality.
- Candidates for water baptism no longer have to be born again.
- Singing is no longer worship. It is now entertainment.
- The testimony service no longer exists. It consumes too much time in our thirty-minute service.
- Midweek prayer meeting is dead. The people are too tired to attend.
- Protracted meetings have become two-day seminars.
- Pastors no longer have to be preachers, just public relations men.
- Pastor's wives set the fashion trend for the ladies of the church. No longer is she an example of Godliness and holiness.
- The world no longer comes to the church when they are tired of the old life and are ready for something new. The church lives like they do.

- The world has become churchy, and the church has become worldly. It's hard to tell where one stops and the other begins.
- Services are omitted for ballgames and county fairs. Easter is a day for a dress parade, not a resurrection.
- Denominations are more interested in being the largest, instead of the holiest.

This kind of church is not ready for the rapture. It will be spewed out. The door of heaven will be shut in its face. The only hope is revival. Real, Holy Ghost, Heaven sent, hell shaking, soul saving revival.

The only hope for revival is that someone catch the vision of a lost generation going to hell and decide to do something about it.

God found them in the past. Surely there must be one, at least one, out there somewhere who can catch the vision and the burden for revival.

- One who would deny self.
- One who would take up his cross and follow Christ.
- One who would forsake all for the glory of God.
- One who would pay the price of revival.

You, dear reader, could be that one. God is not looking for another Finney or Moody. God is looking for you. Hide no longer behind silly reasonings and petty excuses, but say "here am I Lord, send me."

- Sell-out to God.
- Sanctify yourself wholly.
- Fast and pray.
- Turn from evil to God.
- Find the will of God and walk in it—no matter what.
- Give all the glory to God.

Revival will come. Souls will be saved. The name of the Lord will be magnified and a generation will call you blessed.

Lord send a revival. Amen.

Thank you for purchasing *Ghost of Revivals Past*. If you were blessed by this book, consider leaving a review on your favorite retail site, purchasing additional books by this author at WWW.KENNETHGMORRIS.COM, or visiting the publisher's online bookstore at WWW.FILLEDBOOKS.COM.

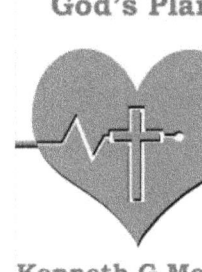

Visit our website to see our entire collection of Pentecostal books.
www.empoweredpublicationsinc.com

www.ingramcontent.com/pod-product-compliance
Lightning Source LLC
Chambersburg PA
CBHW071308040426
42444CB00009B/1935